God is Our Refuge and Our Strength
by George Gipps
with chapters by C. Matthew McMahon

Copyright Information

God is Our Refuge and Our Strength, by George Gipps, with chapters by C. Matthew McMahon
Edited by Susan Ruth and Therese B. McMahon

Copyright © 2021 by Puritan Publications and A Puritan's Mind®

Some language has been updated from the original manuscript. Any change in wording or punctuation has not changed the intent or meaning of the original author(s), and has been made to aid the modern reader.

Published by Puritan Publications
A Ministry of A Puritan's Mind® in Crossville, TN
www.apuritansmind.com
www.puritanpublications.com

All rights reserved. No part of this publication may be reproduced, stored in a retrieval system or transmitted in any form by any means, electronic, mechanical, photocopy, recording or otherwise, without the prior permission of the publisher, except as provided by USA copyright law.

This Print Edition, 2021
Electronic Edition, 2021
Manufactured in the United States of America

ISBN: 978-1-62663-391-9
eISBN: 978-1-62663-390-2

Table of Contents

Submission Under Providence 4
Meet George Gipps 12
God Our Refuge 13
    The Doctrines 17
    Doctrinal Observations 19
    The First Proposition and Doctrine 19
    USE 1 21
    USE 2 22
    USE 3 24
    The Second Proposition and Doctrine 24
    USE 1 31
    The Third Proposition and Doctrine 34
    USE 1 43
    USE 2 45
    USE 3 46
    USE 4 48
Other Helpful Works Published by Puritan Publications
.... 52

Submission Under Providence
by C. Matthew McMahon, Ph.D., Th.D.

George Gipps' work on Psalm 46:1 is a needed remedy for Christians in our day. It is sad that we have only this work by Gipps to peruse, but at the same time, we are thankful to have it. It truly presses the reader (or those who heard him initially preach this sermon to the Assembly) how to seek out God as the Christian's only refuge, strength, help, no matter what is happening providentially in their life. It is a very good question to ask one's self, in placing one's own life under the trial of examination, "How do we *practically submit* under God's sovereignty and providence especially when those providences are hard and trying?"

Certainly, we could quote a great many Scriptures on this topic of submission under providence, especially as it relates to frowning providences, or afflictions. A favorite of mine is Proverbs 16:9, "A man's heart plans his way, But the Lord directs his steps." Gipps uses Psalm 46:1, "God is our refuge and strength, a very present help in trouble." Both are applicable to the question. Of all the theological inquiries a person can ask in their lifetime, the greatest question pondered and prayed over is often, "What is God's will for my life?" And this question, as it relates to affliction, is enhanced greatly at the time one considers it in light of the glory of Christ.

Now, the Bible does not hold a personal record of everything we ought to do day by day in detail for you and I directly. Yes, it houses everything we need for *life and godliness,* but that is not what is meant here. We are rational creatures that like *lists*. It would be most helpful, we think, if God would simply send down a list from heaven for us to follow *as individuals* so that no matter what providential occurrence takes place at a particular time, we have a list to look at and tell us directly what we are to do, how we are to feel and what we should think in such situations. But, God is more *mysterious* than that, and in order to conform his servants into his Son's image and will, (not to just stamp out robots), he gave us *prayer* instead; and prayer is the place Christians run to God as a refuge, strength and help in whatever providential circumstances that occurs. Instead of consulting a list of "do's and don'ts", we are directed to submit our will to his providences through prayer, which means we must be very good at discernment, and very good at godly observation in all his dealings with us. This means, we must know his word in order to do this.

The proverb quoted above is very interesting. It says that a man plans out his ways, but God *directs* his steps. What exactly does *that* mean in the whole consideration of running to the help, refuge and strength of God in prayer? It teaches, simply, we plan out our way, consider our ends, make a strategy for our walk, and God will take care of the rest; in fact, God takes care of all those who seek the Kingdom of heaven first, and all other things "shall be added unto them." This "seems" easy enough to do. We do this everyday, *so we think*. We choose what to wear, what to eat, what time we will make it to work and various other common things that comprise our particular day. Maybe we even plan out our entire week, or plan out what will happen in the next 6 months based on our financial situation. Our inner man (our heart, soul and mind) plans out or devises the steps we would *like* to take throughout our life. Yet, it is God who actually directs our steps. This seems to place a *mystery* into the practical observations of daily life. It is interesting that in this proverb the word "directs" (that which the Lord accomplishes) is to, "set firm or establish." In other words, though a man, in the inner recesses of his heart, soul and mind "plans his way" it is the Lord who actually *establishes* the path on a solid foundation on which he is to walk. That means that if we plan something he does not establish, or that we sin in some instance in some besetting sin or presumptuous sin, we are fighting *against* his divine will. Again, we do not have a list that says "at 35 years of age you will take such and such a job." And "at 40 years of age, you will buy this or that car, and move to this or that city." All of those decisions fall under the realm of Christian prudence, and rightly applying principles that we glean from the Bible to direct our life in wisdom and truth under God's sovereign providence. Yet, what do we do in planning out our way and our steps when there are afflicting providences abounding in our life? This complicates the issue.

Sometimes God directs us on paths we do not necessarily like, but he does so for the very reason that he desires us to come to him for help, strength and refuge. It may be that we are Joseph in prison, or Moses in Midian.

We are hiding out in Egypt for a while like Mary and Joseph, because circumstances dictate such. Sometimes God brings us through dark days on purpose, like Job on the ash heap, and sometimes he brings us through beams of heavenly light (we like those days *better*). Whatever the providences that God directs us in as his people and children, we ought to take consolation in that he is ordering all things for his glory, and looking out for our best interest as those elected in the *Beloved Christ*. Romans 8:28 is a most famous verse on this, "And we know that all things work together for good to them that love God, to them who are the called according to his purpose." Do we "know" this? Or are we just acquiescing to the Stoic disposition of a frowning providence when trials come along? Do we really "know" God is looking out for our good? Do we really think he loves us even amidst afflictions? Do we know that he has our best interest in mind if we are called according to his purposes? Are we truly, in those difficult times, then, running to the strong Tower of his power and wisdom, and is he our ever-present help, strength and refuge? Sometimes we live as though *we do not know*. We think that because we have planned out certain steps, and want to take a certain path, that when such a path crumbles before our eyes and that hard and trying circumstances comes our way, we quickly assume that God has forsaken us, that he is mad at us, that he is chastising us, that he is frowning on us (yes, it *could* be that, but we have a disposition to *always* think the worst). In this way, Christians are very fickle people. They are often tossed *to and fro* in the winds of God's providential directions and they feel like a buoy thrown around on the waves of indifference. They forget, though, that the buoy is anchored to the bottom of the ocean and will not really be moved, though it may *feel* like it at the time, because the anchor is Jesus Christ. They forget all about Psalm 46:1.

A minister said to me once, "We must make a difference between plans that are godly, and plans that are God's." How true this is. It may be a godly plan that you have devised. Maybe you are contemplating a new job. Maybe you are thinking about marriage and having children. Maybe you are thinking about teaching in a church, or going into the ministry. It could be just about any *thing* a Christian could plan out to do, with some God glorifying end to it all. But there is a great difference between what is a godly plan, and what is God's plan. Would it have been a godly thing to do for Joseph's brothers *not* to throw him in a pit or sell him into slavery? Would it have been a godly thing for king Solomon *not* to take for himself many wives? Would it have been a godly thing for Paul to go into Phrygia to preach the Gospel? Men can *plan out* godly plans, but that does not mean such plans are always God's plans, (and make note: there is no excuse in such plans for any kind of sin). Rest assured, all of God's plans are godly plans, but not all godly plans are God's plans. That is somewhat of a tongue twister, but it should also be a heart wrenching truth embedded in every Christian. Christians submit to God's providence, whether they like that providence, or whether it is an afflicting or frowning one. We are not simply to follow godly plans we like, but *God's plans* for us; both must be matched up together and discerned. He is the One who establishes our plans and makes them stand firm. He is the One who providentially oversees the continuity of those plans. And in all those plans, and in all the sovereign orderings of all things in our life, we are to hold steadfastly to Christ, and Christ alone as our present help, strength and refuge. This is what Gipps will show in considering Psalm 46:1.

We search the scriptures and learn and live out the principles they teach. This is what godly Christians *desire* to do. They hold fast to those principles to form a godly plan under the providence of God throughout their life; this makes them discerning, makes them to take heed, and often makes them wise. We are sure God will bless those plans and course of action because such a course is godly. But, your godly plan may be nothing like God's plan, his ordering of specific events for your life and for your good. Your plan has a destination that you are seeking, a payoff, success, fruit – and there is nothing wrong with that; but the purpose of God's plan is to change us and conform us into the image of Christ. We are being transformed into the *very image of Christ* day by day. In this we run to him always as our very present help, strength and refuge ... or do we? We will think and act more like him if we do, we will realize and eventually hold onto nothing except *Christ and him crucified*. But are you relying on what *you hope and like*, or *what is best for you?* If you get boils all over your body, will you say with Job, "Though he slay me, yet will I trust in him"? Or is it that you only trust in him when you think things are going well?

You have a plan for your life, and it didn't include cancer. Will you still trust God with your cancer nonetheless?

There are some very poignant Scriptures which bear out this "neediness" of the Christian to Jesus Christ as they work out their sanctification by walking in the Spirit under God's directing providence. Consider these: "And he said unto me, My grace is sufficient for thee: for my strength is made perfect in weakness. Most gladly therefore will I rather glory in my infirmities, that the power of Christ may rest upon me," (2 Corinthians 12:9). "My help cometh from the LORD, which made heaven and earth," (Psalm 121:2). "But we had the sentence of death in ourselves, that we should not trust in ourselves but in God which raiseth the dead: Who delivered us from so great a death, and doth deliver: in whom we trust that He will yet deliver us," (2 Corinthians 1:9-10). "...greater is He that is in you, than He that is in the world," (1 John 4:4). "And God is able to make all grace abound toward you; that ye, always having all sufficiency in all things, may abound to every good work," (2 Corinthians 9:8). "Then spake Jesus again unto them, saying, I am the light of the world: he that followeth me shall not walk in darkness, but shall have the light of life," (John 8:12). "And he said "the LORD is my rock, and my fortress, and my deliverer," (2 Sam. 22:2). "Humble ourselves therefore under the mighty hand of God, that He may exalt you in due time," (1 Peter 5:6). "I can do all things through Christ which strengtheneth me," (Philippians 4:13). And yes, Gipps' text is quite profitable in this, "God is our refuge and strength, a very pleasant help in trouble," (Psalm 46:1).

In bearing in mind these truths, Gipps will press you, reader, to ruminate in the need to be submissive to God in his providence. It is the truth, that it is the portion of God's church and children to find in this life very great and abundant troubles. What do they do when they find such trouble? It is the wisdom of God's church and children to make God their hope, refuge, and shelter in *all* their troubles. And if they are providentially placed in affliction, frowning providences, or planning out a way that seems right to them to navigate life under God's providence, then, it is the comfort of God's church and children who trust in him that they shall find God a very present, strong, and abundant help in all their troubles no matter what they are. This work is a blessed help in considering this, and directing your steps in the right and godly way.

There is a *caveat* here with Gipps. It surrounds the words "who trust in him." If a professing believer does not actually trust in God, they cannot rightly be said to seek him as their very present *help, strength and refuge.* Gipps will make this distinction very clear. But for those who are born again, truly children of the Great King Jesus, they can go to him in all of life's various questions and difficulties, and trust that their steps are directed in the best possible manner by the God who is their eternal and unchangeable help, strength and refuge.

In Christ's grace and mercy,
C. Matthew McMahon, Ph.D., Th.D.
From my study, January 11, 2021.

Meet George Gipps
Edited by C. Matthew McMahon, Ph.D., Th.D.

Little is known about Rev. George Gipps B.A. (n.d.) (sometimes spelled Gippes). He was a minister in Leicester-shire, a county in the center of England. He earned his B.A. from St. John's College, Cambridge, in 1610; and earned his M.A. July, 10, 1621. He became the canon of Lichfield in 1624, rector of St. Andrew, Hertford, in the same year, and minister of Aylstone later in 1633. He subsequently resigned the latter post, and was sequestered to that of Bottesford, Leicester, in 1646.[1]

He is noted as a strong Christian of piety, and a masterful student of various cases on conscience, and how to remedy them according to the word of God. He was chosen as one of the Westminster Assembly of Divines and is noted by Daniel Neal as one who constantly attended. He preached in the house of commons, on November 27th on a fast day, on the text of this volume, Psalm 46:1. Of any other works, we have no notation, and no other pieces have survived of his to this day.

---

[1] See Foster's *Index Eccl. & Add. MS.* 15,670, p. 29.

God Our Refuge[2]

Psalm 46:1, "God is our refuge and strength, a very present help in trouble."

Being the first verse of this 46th Psalm, it is independent from any preceding passage. Rather than troubling you with the title, I will begin this message with Luther's comment on this Psalm. In his words, "It is a thanksgiving to God for his wonderful benefits, in keeping his church safe from all the enemies of it, those nations which circled them in on every side, who both in hostile and treacherous manner sought their utmost ruin. This therefore the Jews sang to support their faith, and to raise their fainting spirits in all their extremities: which also," (he adds), "let us now sing to the honor of God, powerfully and miraculously preserving his word and church by this Psalm. It explains things against the errors and heresies of giddy brained spirits. Against the power and policy of cruel tyrants. Against the baits of sin, the world, and the flesh, and against all malice of Satan by all his engineers."

For all these reasons, this psalm is perfectly suited to our present times, as well as to those former times and conditions. Therefore, according to my usual method, I will proceed to propose these three things. 1. Explication of the sense of the words. 2. Observation of their doctrinal truths. 3. Application of it to our own souls.

---

[2] A Sermon Preached to the Honorable House of Commons on their Monthly Fast November 27, 1644.

We begin with the *explication* of the words in order.

The first word, "God," is the same God whom Luke describes in Acts 17:24, "that made the world, and all things therein: that dwelleth not in temples made with hands." This is that same God "in whom we live and move and have our being," (Acts 17:28). This is the first word.

The second word is "is," as we read it. Other translations read "shall be." And still others read simply, "God our refuge," (including the original text). All these differing readings give us the full sense of God. Regarding his nature, God *is*; resolvedly, God *shall be;* experientially, God *our refuge*, which is an exclamation with exultation. These are ravished affections utter broken sentences with elevated voice, disregarding rules of grammar. Experience of God's past mercies give birth to resolution for the time to come, resulting in an exultation of the heart in admiration of God's mercy. Let this suffice for the second word.

The third word is "our," which some read affixed to God, in this way *our God;* others to refuge, in this way give the meaning *God is our refuge*. Both together they give the full sense, which is, "Our God is our refuge." First, God becomes our God by covenant, then he becomes our refuge by claim. This suffices for the third word.

The fourth word is "refuge," as we read it. In other places it is rendered "hope", and still others, "shelter." Here is the difference between these renderings. Hope is that grace in our hearts which connects us to our *refuge* by which we arrive at a shelter to repose ourselves in. All three readings join together to make up the full sense, in this way, "A heart rightly anchored by hope in God, may safely fly unto him, and by so doing, securely shelter himself in him." Henry Ainsworth, a leader of the ancient church, said that "God will be to us a hopeful shelter, and a strength, a help in distresses we shall find very great..." This will suffice for the fourth word.

The fifth word is "strength," which indicates not just strength in the concrete sense, but also in the abstract – an absolute, infinite, and all-sufficient strength. And as such, it may look either backward to shelter, or forward to help. Both are most full. In this way, God is so all sufficient in strength that those who fly to him for shelter shall certainly have help from him.

The sixth word as it appears in the original text is "help" or *helper*. The former signifies the quality, the latter the person so qualified. And both in one make up our fullness or comfort. God who undertakes is fully gifted and qualified for what he undertakes, in contrast to many who bear the name of what they have no skill to perform.

The seventh word is "trouble," or "troubles," in many of the several readings. The former represents the singular number, pertaining to *each and any single trouble whatsoever*, the latter the plural number (from the Septuagint) pertaining to collectively, *in all troubles doubled and multiplied however many they may be.*

The eighth, or last word (or rather phrase) is "very present," as we read it. But the original language with diverse translations include the verb "find," indicating, "we shall find very present, great, abundant, yes, too, too present, great and abundant." And all these several readings do not include the full variety of their expositions that Augustine and generally the ancients followed. So, in the full sense, we consider it this way, "we shall find God a very present, yes, too, *too* present, great and abundant help for too, *too* present, great and abundant troubles which we shall find."

A third sort join both ideas in one, and take all this together, as the most full sense, in this way, "God's saints in this life are sure to find very present, great and abundant troubles, yes, too great for them to bear, but their comfort is that they are as sure to find God a very present, great and abundant help in all their troubles, yes, too great to be overcome by them."

Give me leave to add one thing more to complete the sense, and so put an end to the first general part which is the explication of the words. As the original Hebrew text expressed no verb at all, neither *is*, nor *shall be*, nor any other, why do we supply any? When we string all the words of our text on this verb, *find* (which does appear in the Hebrew) and let it run through them all, making one entire rich chain, it reads "we shall find God our refuge, strength and very present help in trouble." This is the explanation of the text.

The Doctrines

Now let us look to the second point, an observation of these doctrinal truths which follow.

First, we own that only one God made all things (Acts 17).

Second, we should not rest until we have made this God our God, by his most sure and firm covenant.

Third, once this is done, we may securely anchor our hope in him.

Fourth, with our hope anchored in him, we may in all straights and troubles fly to him.

Fifth, when we fly to him, he will give us shelter and harbor.

Sixth, this is no questionable, tottering shelter, but a shelter of strength which is all sufficient.

Seventh, at the same time, this shelter does not keep us from *finding troubles* very present, great, and abundant, that are beyond our strength to bear.

Eighth, nevertheless, we have this comfort, that in all of them we are sure to find God a more present, great and abundant helper, most able and willing to help us through.

Ninth, this promise is ours if we keep ourselves free from sin by repentance. Otherwise, we will be found out through an accusing conscience.

Tenth, and even in this we find comfort, that on our repentance for the most heinous sins, we will be met with God's pardon and forgiveness. And as we are of the election of grace, we shall be brought by God to repentance and salvation.

Lastly, to help us combine these all into one whole, let us gather experiments of what is past to settle our resolution for that which is to come, and from both testify with elevation of both heart and voice that, "We shall find God our refuge, and strength, a very present help in trouble."

This text is full of comfort, if we are as full of faith to use it with the best advantage to our souls. Though however excellent all these divine truths are, and however plentifully these differing readings from God's Word abound, I prefer to contain my thoughts within its plain song, shared with you in these three following *propositions*.

First, it is the portion of God's church and his children to find in and through this life very present (yes, even "too, *too* present") great and abundant troubles that must be waded through.

Second, it is the wisdom of God's church and children to make God their hope, refuge, and shelter in all these troubles.

Third, it is the comfort of God's church and children, that in so doing they shall find God a very present (yes, "too, *too* present") great and abundant help in all these troubles.

We have now covered this first branch, namely, the explication of the sense of the words, and are ready to move unto the second branch which is that of the doctrinal observations, their use and application.

Doctrinal Observations

These three points are so naturally linked together that a great many texts of Scripture reiterate them. For example, the Psalm 18 passage does so generally throughout. And more particularly, verse 4, "The sorrows of death compassed me, the floods of ungodly men made me afraid," in this is the first point. Verse 2, "My God, my rock, my fortress, my strength, my buckler, my high tower, in whom I will trust," in this is the second point. Verse 3, "I will call upon the Lord, so shall I be saved from mine enemies," and verse 48, "He delivers me from mine enemies," therein is the third point. Another example is Psalm 34:19, "Many are the afflictions of the righteous," (the first point) "but the Lord delivered him out of them all," (the third point), and verse 22, "None that trust in him shall be desolate," (the second and third point jointly). As this is so frequently the case elsewhere in Scripture, we shall occasionally reference them in our following discourse.

The First Proposition and Doctrine

And now we enter our first proposition, which is that it is the portion of God's church and children to find in this life very great and abundant troubles. The ratifying of this truth shall be noted first in a brief numbering of these troubles. Secondly, in deducing certain conclusions which are, 1) the troubles in this life are either temporal or spiritual, and, 2) temporal includes life itself, death, pains, and sickness; poverty with its accompanying lack of convenient meat, drink, clothing, and dwelling; infamy and its accompanying scorn, disgrace, contempt, and slander. Spiritual troubles include that inbred sexual desire, that snake in our bosom and its accompanying temptations to actual sins, too many presumptions which often lead to gross scandal, resulting in spiritual desertion and God giving us up to Satan's buffetings.

It is important to note that all these evils are common to all Adam's offspring, both godly and wicked alike in this life (Eccl. 9:1-2). And as Job 5:7 says, "Man is born into trouble as the sparks fly upward." Secondly, this common condition did not flow from our creation by God's sovereign right of dominion but is an act of God's justice upon Adam's fall. As a result of Adam's sin, God's passed punishment on all his posterity, by which the whole world of creatures is cursed. "In the day thou eat of it thou shalt surely die," (Gen. 2:17). Thirdly, the consequence of these results in a vast difference between the godly and the wicked, even as vast as there is distance between the highest heaven and the lowest hell. Matthew 25:32 says the two shall be separated as goats and sheep. "Come ye blessed," (verse 34), and "Depart ye cursed," (verse 41), and "the righteous shall go into life eternal and the wicked into everlasting punishment," (verse 46). The great trouble for the ungodly is their temporal evils, as they are insensible of spiritual ones. They never tire of sin, but desire to be able to sin infinitely while enjoying all the accommodations of life and their lusts, regardless of their internal hell of conscience and the infernal hell of torments to follow. The godly, on the other hand, consider living in sin to be the most hellish condition, and perfect holiness as the apex of their eternal happiness. And thirdly, the wicked could be content never to see God's face and enjoy his favor in heaven so that they might never see his frown and feel his wrath in hell; the righteous, on the other hand, acknowledge God's favor better than life itself, in whose presence is fulness of joy, and at whose right hand are pleasures for evermore.

Let this suffice for the Doctrinal part of this first Proposition.

USE 1

Use 1. The first use we address here is to answer the question, "why will God be so harsh to his own children, as this doctrine indicates?" The answer is twofold. First, it may seem that he is subjecting his children to a common condition with others in the kinds of their sufferings. However, this is not so, for God takes special care of his own in all their sufferings for their spiritual and eternal good. A second answer is that God's providence works best with his most wise dispensation. In other words, if the godly totally escaped suffering and only the wicked experienced troubles, such multitudes of mercenaries would profess to be Christians that sincerity would not be discerned nor valued. The fact that we must suffer many tribulations to enter the kingdom of heaven staves off hypocrites. Satan was not impressed with Job's service to God as long as God protected him (Job 1:9), but thought that afflictions would have staggered and shattered his faith (though Job proves him wrong, which was a great foil to Satan). So, quite often God sends Christians into trials to see if they will continue to embrace their faith merely and entirely for the sake of Christ. And on the contrary, if the wicked escaped suffering and only the godly were troubled, this would discourage God's children and encourage wickedness. Knowing this, how did Job's friends accuse him of being a hypocrite when God had so afflicted him? And why is it that when the church suffers, it prospers? This possibility moved patient Moses to be unrelenting in his request to God that he not destroy Israel in the wilderness, lest the Egyptians should say that God brought them out of Egypt for mischief, to slay them in the mountains, or that he was not able to bring them into Canaan (Exod. 32:11-12; Num. 14:16). Therefore, God's wisdom orders it, that his justice shall be satisfied by all suffering similar troubles, and his grace and mercy shown by so sanctifying troubles for his children's good.

USE 2

A second *use* is exhortation, that we do not shun troubles when God sends them, but patiently embrace and approve them. Had we in our own country sympathized with the churches in other countries (Germany and France), (and more lately of Ireland and Scotland), by prayers and tears and aide for them according to their necessities and our abilities, most probably we might have escaped this fierce storm that is now pouring down upon our own country (Ezek. 9:4-6; Amos 6:1, 3, 6-7; Matt. 11:17). But regrettably, we are so far from sharing with our brethren's sufferings that we will not own that general charge of all Christians to be crucified to the world, and the world to us. For as yet in our most sad present condition, even when summoned to mourning and fasting, we prefer to please ourselves with the vain delights of the world. As the kingdom of heaven does not focus on meat and drink, pomp and pleasure, or other temporary and earthly satisfactions, so the heirs of this kingdom should not be so taken with them (Matt. 6:32-33). Christ tells us to seek the interests of the kingdom of God first, and all these earthly needs will be given you. You will never have to stoop or strain to gain such empty delights. Not that we are not worthy of the world, but that it is not worthy of us. Not that these things are too good for us, but as kingdom children we are too honorable to place our affections on them. Christ states that our inner nature is evidenced by our outer fruits. Just as the herbalist can distinguish each plant, not only by its fruit but by its leaves, so also, our outward behaviors distinguish the children of the kingdom of God from those in the kingdom of Satan.

USE 3

I add a third use, a further exhortation, that we make and keep *covenant* with God to be our God, and not break covenant with him, so he will not break with us. Faith, fear, love, and universal obedience to his whole revealed will is the only effectual means to keep us from the world and under the protection of his covenant, "But if from thence thou shalt seek the LORD thy God, thou shalt find him, if thou seek him with all thy heart and with all thy soul. When thou art in tribulation, and all these things are come upon thee, even in the latter days, if thou turn to the LORD thy God, and shalt be obedient unto his voice; (For the LORD thy God is a merciful God;) he will not forsake thee, neither destroy thee, nor forget the covenant of thy fathers which he sware unto them," (Deut. 4:29-31).

The Second Proposition and Doctrine

So now I pass to the second Proposition, namely, that it is the wisdom of God's church and children to make God their hope, refuge, and shelter in all their troubles. To the proof of Scripture I gave you in the general discussion of all three doctrines, we shall now add the demonstrative grounds of reason, which are these two. First, because in God is full, certain, and sufficient help in all troubles.

Secondly, because apart from God, in no creature, no not in all the creatures, is there full, certain, and sufficient help. If these two are as strongly confirmed as they are easily affirmed, I am sure you cannot question their validity. Instinct of nature teaches every creature to fly for shelter when it needs help (Psa. 104:18, Proverbs 30:26), as both David and Solomon tell us how the conies fly to the holes of the rocks and the goats to the steep craggy tops of it. Our only work, therefore, is to make good these two reasons.

Outside of God, among all the creatures in the universe not one can offer full, certain, and sufficient help, for these three *reasons.*

Reason 1: First, all creatures are instrumental subservient helps under God, in and for God, how, and how far he pleases. He stops, turns, re-routes, and overturns them all at his pleasure. Therefore, in them and outside of him no safe repose for help exists. Lions, fire, water, winds, seas, and even devils and all the hosts of creatures are wholly at his beck and call. He instructs one to go, and he goes, another to stay and he stays. As the centurion said to Christ, "say the word only, and my servant will be whole." We have plenty of Scripture to show this in particular, and we shall mention some of them.

Reason 2: The second reason is because these instrumental helps are only partial and particular, some in one kind, some in another, but none in all. They cannot all join in one sufficient help in all troubles, though God blesses and enables them to act and work. In the first creation, as well as in Noah's flood, the waters covered the surface of the whole earth and would perpetually do so if God did not design it for the good of man. For without the atmosphere we would all smother without air to breathe. Fire heats and dries, but it also burns and consumes. Water moistens and cools, but it also sinks and drowns as God determines. God made all the elements in his creation fruitful and serviceable for the use of man.

But some may object that if God blesses and enables each creature to do his part, can they not all jointly supply sufficient help in all our wants and needs?

Answer. First, it is more wise, safe, generous, and comfortable to go immediately and directly to God, than secondarily to the creatures for help, for this is both a short cut and the more secure way, especially since God has so graciously invited us, "Call upon me in the day of trouble, I will deliver thee, and thou shalt glorify me." Who begs the keeper for a piece of venison if he has free access to ask for all the meat he wants from the Master of the game?

A second answer is because God reserves for himself his royal power to underwrite all the workings of all his creatures. God presently withdraws his blessing from the creature when man ignores the Creator and begins to depend on the creature. As it was with the prodigal son in the gospel, who on receiving his portion from his father, went into a far country and spent all he had. He only returned to the father when he was hungry and had no food.

Necessity moves us to seek the resources we need from God and to delight in him daily. This is why Christ's exemplary prayer teaches us to pray, "Give us this day our daily bread," not to inform him of our needs, because he knows them better than we do. Nor is it to urge him to supply our needs, who is more ready to give than we are to ask. He is not advantaged by our service, to whom the whole creation can add nothing, neither does he lack anything. But merely and purely in mercy and grace he will have us see him as the source of our supply, "For every creature of God is good, and nothing to be refused, if it be received with thanksgiving: for it is sanctified by the word of God and prayer," (1 Tim. 4:4-5). He also wants to initiate in us his saints and servants a delight to converse with him as he did with Adam in paradise, to establish us in our new creation. How much greater is one's sin who neglects such great grace offered them!

Take the third and last answer to the objection, namely again that it is not so; because God reserves some choicest blessings for himself immediately to bestow on his children without the help of any creature and beyond the course of nature. These are namely, election, redemption, justification, sanctification and glorification, with all spiritual gifts. So if we choose to run to any creature for aid, whether glorified saint or angel, or even to our own merits, we make void the grace of God. Psalm 73:25-26 says, "Whom have I in heaven but thee, and there is none in earth that I desire besides thee... God is the strength of my heart and my portion forever."

And if any shall here further object, God uses his ministry and ordinances as means on his behalf. To be sure, these means are not natural within the compass of creation, but supernatural, directly from God and from heaven specifically for those ends. These means work supernaturally and arbitrarily, not naturally and necessarily. In other words, they only work when, where, and how God pleases. And when they do, it is not a result of any infused inherent quality in them, but rather from God, by the concurrence of his grace and our obedience of faith in him. Fire burns and water wets by virtue of inherent qualities given them from God. Therefore they all burn and wet all alike. But by one man's ministry a creature is converted, when not by others, because of the gracious pleasure of our good God. As it is said in 1 Corinthians 2:3, "I was with you in weakness, and in fear, and in much trembling." And, "my preaching was not with enticing words of man's wisdom, but in demonstration of the spirit and power," (verse 4). "That your faith should not stand in the wisdom of men, but in the power of God," (verse 5). "You see your calling, that not many wise, mighty, noble," *etc.* (verse 27). But God uses the foolish and weak things of the world to confound the wise and mighty (verse 31) that he that glories should glory (verse 29) only in the Lord. Rom. 9:15 states, "I will have mercy on whom I will have mercy." Verse 16 says that it is not in him that wills, nor in him that runs, but in God that shows mercy (see also verse 18). And whom he will, he hardens. And in Acts 16, about the woman to whom the apostles preached (among many who heard them), Scripture says that "the Lord opened her heart," (Acts 16:14).

Finally, God often infuses grace without using any means, as in those he sanctifies in and from the womb like John the Baptist, those above and contrary to means, as in the thief converted on the cross, and in those like Saul, who in the heat of pursuit of the saints in order to persecute them was himself made a chief one, a choice one. Indeed, God has brought about many miracles, even in natural and civil affairs of men that are contrary to natural principles, to demonstrate his sovereignty and to show us that we may go to and rest wholly on him, and not on the creature.

The third and final reason for the clearing of this doctrine follows. As the creature is only God's instrument (the first reason), and no more than a partial and particular help (the second reason), so at best it is a creature full of vanity, emptiness, and deceit, and will fail us most when we most rely on it. This is why the Scripture frequently reminds us that it is a lie, and feeds lies to those who fly to it. "We have made lies our refuge, and have hid ourselves under falsehood," (Isa. 28:15). "The hail shall sweep away the refuge of lies," (verse 17). "O Lord my strength, my fortress, my refuge in the day of affliction, surely our fathers have inherited lies," (Jer. 16:19). The antithesis is between God and all things, between vanity and things in which there is no profit. So either the creature is a mere natural agent, without free choice, and God curses the creature which proves to be a lie to us because we trusted in it (*i.e.,* he makes the earth as iron and heaven as brass to us). On the other hand, if the creature is a voluntary agent (as men and angels) then it often proves to be a lie to us maliciously, as wicked men and devils act as servants to the god of this world. Another option is that if they are good men, they prove a lie to us through weakness, (forgetfulness or other weakness), attempting to undertake something that is above their strength and in so doing frustrate their good intentions.

And this, beloved, is the most candid interpretation that we attribute to a very many of our present state affairs. We trust their failings are from human frailty and not from devilish malice and treachery. Of course, there are those that offend out of malicious wickedness. But God will find those out and call them into account.

Lastly, even good angels prove a lie to us, not by any malice or weakness in them, but because we place and force our hopes on them, promising ourselves more from them than they are capable of doing, more than they dare or can promise to do for us. Though truly in this case we prove to be a lie unto ourselves, by placing our trust in the creatures, which they would not have us do. The papists here again are miserably hindered because of their emphasis on the adoration and invocation of the glorified saints and angels. Observe the example of John who, when falling at the angel's feet to worship him, the angel said, "See thou do it not: I am thy fellow servant, and of thy brethren that have the testimony of Jesus. Worship God..." (Rev. 19:10, 22:9). The Scripture abundantly charges us not to trust our own wits, wisdom, wills, wealth, strength, favor of princes, multitude of people, or whatever other being in creation. We are not to trust even our Christian goodness, for this is also an aspect of creation. And in this you have the demonstration of our second doctrine: that the whole creature is vanity and a lie to trust in. Therefore, it is the wise saint who flies to and relies on God alone in all their troubles.

Though we should never fix our trust elsewhere, yet even this consideration alone questions (or rather denies) God's all wise, just, good, and powerful providence. For if we did truly believe he is all these and more to us, we would certainly trust in him. "O my God, I trust in thee: let me not be ashamed, let not mine enemies triumph over me," (Psalm 25:2). And yet the common curse of these times is that we trust God no further than we see him. And in so doing we forsake our first love and the cause of Christ which we were converted to.

USE 1

But then much more are those to be reproved who look to anything or anyone else to trust instead of God. Why is it so hard for us to simply trust God? I answer that, first, we are all so swayed by our physical senses that we live totally in and for the present, counting one bird in the hand of more value than two in the bush – though it is that bush of Moses which burned and was not consumed (Exod. 3:2-3; Deut. 33:16), and though we have God's assurance that for all our thorny perplexities we have his wise and gracious providence to, at length, remove us out of them and set us at liberty so that they do not consume us; and still, we fail to call on him.

A second way we distrust God and trust in the creature instead is by not seeking repose in him, which esteems and honors him. On the contrary, we think, talk, and dote wholly in the worth of our counselors. "You say 'today or tomorrow we will go into such a city, and continue there a year, and buy and sell, and get gain.' Whereas you know not what shall be on the morrow. For what is your life? It is even a vapor, that appears for a little time, and then vanishes away. For that you ought to say, 'If the Lord will, we shall live, and do this, or that,'" (James 4:13-16).

Therefore, God will remove our idols from us, if he intends good to us, as he has already removed some of our prime counselors in order to teach us to trust in him, the living Lord, who never fails those that trust in him.

A third and last application is to hope in and fly wholly to God in all our troubles. As Lamentations 3:24-26 states, "The Lord is my portion, saith my soul, therefore will I hope in him. The Lord is good to them that wait for him, that seek him. It is good that we should hope and quietly wait for the salvation of the Lord." I shall drive home this exhortation by offering *four rules* which may serve both as the means directing us and as marks determining whether we do or not.

Rule 1: (which is both directive and detective), 1. Seek to gain a right knowledge and esteem of God in all his attributes of power, wisdom, truth, goodness, mercy and providence, first from his word, and then from your own observation. And if you have not yet attained the latter, then choose to trust him on his bare word, which so honors God that he will make it good to you sooner or later in your experience. "They that know thy name," (that is to say, "thy attributes") "will put their trust in thee, for thou Lord hast not forsaken them that seek thee," (Psa. 9:10).

Rule 2. Learn to trust God freely and fully. Trust in nothing else without or above, nothing but him (Psa. 44:6-8). "Trust in the Lord with all thy heart, and lean not to thine own understanding," (Proverbs 3:5).

Rule 3. Trust in God constantly, always, in all difficulties and improbabilities, in your greatest extremities, in your greatest securities. In all conditions. When you possess all those things that the world trusts in, still do not look to those things but to God. And when you have nothing that those of the world trust in, yet even then rest in him securely. Happy is that man who trusts in God in all occurrences whatsoever. For I am certain that a true hope and trust in God would bear us up against the most mountainous troubles that can befall us (Psa. 62:5-8).

Rule 4. Trust in God perpetually, to death and even in death itself. This is proper to the believer, who has hope in death, in contrast to all the world's hopes which perish at death. This made the blood of the martyrs a true seed to the church because those who did not obey the word were won without the word when they beheld the martyrs' resolution coupled with the fear of God. And so, devoid of the fear of death, they were convinced of a more glorious estate after death which positioned them to hear instruction, and so often led to their saving conversion. And in the interim, they rest in perfect bliss, free from sin and sorrow, expecting a glorious resurrection. In this regard, they are likened in Scripture to seed (1 Cor. 15). "Trust in the Lord Jehovah forever, for in him is everlasting strength," (Isa. 26:4). "Though he kills me, yet will I trust in him," (Job 13:15).

The Third Proposition and Doctrine

Let this suffice for the second proposition; and so, pass we to the third and last. The Doctrine is: that it is the comfort of God's church and children who trust in him that they shall find God a very present, strong, and abundant help in all their troubles no matter what they are. The proof has, in part, been made good in the second point. But to further clarify, I shall first gather up the gradual arguments in our text.

1. God is our hope, refuge, and shelter; our hope makes us fly to him for shelter. Unlike some who, in a storm, hasten to shelter under a tree which so beats them with rain that they leave it and instead choose to expose themselves to the weather, God is the all sufficient one who protects those who make him their shelter. As men are more able than willing to help, the text adds that we will find God to be, "a help that is ready and willing." Also, our text states that in very great and abundant troubles,

even when we find them too, *too* great and abundant, still he will bear us through them and out of them all.

It is easy to show you particular experiences from Scripture which your own observation may supply, in both temporal and spiritual troubles, but I choose rather to remove a trivial objection which argues against this truth.

Objection: Experience tells us that the godly are overrun with troubles, and they sink and perish under them. I shall give you a sevenfold answer to this objection.

Answer 1. The troubles that befall us in this life are common to both godly and wicked men, nevertheless God helps the godly through and out of them all.

Answer 2. In order to uphold the harmony of these two truths and to contain each of them within its bounds, we must remind ourselves of the distinction between temporal troubles that have to do with our natural life and spiritual troubles that relate to our supernatural life. We should consider the difference between both the matter and the manner of these differing kinds of troubles. The matter is the *kind* of troubles we suffer, such as sickness, hunger, thirst, nakedness, death, Satan's temptations, *etc.* The manner is *God's regard* for the man who is troubled, and man's respect back again to God.

From here we can draw four conclusions. The first is that no matter how temporal troubles are for both the godly and the wicked, in their manner they are sanctified to the godly and not to the wicked. The godly have a personal relationship with the sovereign God who is the author of all circumstances, so they can rectify their troubles with the providence of God. With God as their Father, they are suited to bear troubles as correction or chastisement from the Father. They are able to wean themselves from the love of this world, which is full of trouble. Being children of God, they hate sin and desire to mortify sin which is the primary cause of all trouble by laboring for holiness and looking for a better life in eternity with God. And all this makes them hope all the more in the God whom they fly to for help, and learn with David to say, "Before I was afflicted, I went astray: but now have I kept thy Word. I know, O Lord, that thy judgments are right, and that thou in faithfulness hast afflicted me," (Psa. 119:67, 75). In regard to God's children, the delivery of all temporal troubles is conditional, not absolute, namely, when, how, and how far God's wisdom sees best for his glory and their good.

A second conclusion is that the spiritual trouble of sin, however it may look alike in both the godly and the wicked in substance, yet for its manner it is quite different. The godly sin due to infirmity, not because of presumption. Their sins are more immediate violations, not contrived beforehand. They are regretted, not boasted in afterward. They do not *willingly* serve them. Sin does not reign in the heart of the godly and therefore is not sin, "unto death." All this is quite the opposite with the wicked. Because they are all flesh, sin finds no opposition in them. But the godly are both flesh and Spirit. "For the flesh lusteth against the Spirit, and the Spirit against the flesh: and these are contrary the one to the other: so that ye cannot do the things that ye would," (Gal. 5:17). They are, therefore, continually at war with the sin that they experience. In this way the godly cannot totally, or finally sink under sin, because the Spirit cannot be subdued and conquered by the flesh. "Ye are of God, little children, and have overcome them: because greater is he that is in you, then he that is in the world," (1 John 4:4).

A third conclusion is that though God allows his children to be shrewdly buffeted by Satan for trial and chastisement, yet despair cannot totally or finally prevail over them, for they shall recover, and God's grace shall be sufficient for them.

The fourth and last conclusion is that however difficult it may be with the godly in this life, yet the end of the righteous outshines it all, as Paul says in 2 Timothy 4:7-8, "I have fought a good fight. I have finished the course. I have kept the faith. Henceforth is laid up for me a crown of righteousness, and not to me only, but to those also that love his appearing." And, "Who shall separate us from the love of Christ? shall tribulation, or distress, or persecution, or famine, or nakedness, or peril, or sword?" (Rom. 8:35). The final condition of the wicked, to the contrary, is that they will sink without help under all these troubles throughout all eternity.

But here may some object, as noted in John 11:37, "Could not this man, which opened the eyes of the blind, have caused that even this man should not have died?" So, could not God have prevented man's fall into sin and misery and so Christ's death? Or at least by his death could

God not have perfectly freed his children from all sin and misery?

Let us hear Paul's answer. "O man, who art thou that disputes with God?" Most assuredly, an all-powerful God could have done it, if in his infinite wisdom he had seen it best to do so. These are depths we cannot fathom to its bottom, yet we can dive into the deep end of the following five truths.

First, God is of absolute infinite perfection from all eternity, needing no creation nor creature to add anything to him.

Secondly, though the whole creation may seem merely arbitrary, yet it is all working in sync with some end suitable to his excellency and worthy of his undertakings. As every wise man will have a valuable, determined end in his actions, much more will God in his infinite wisdom so order it.

Thirdly, as a result, God's end can be none other than the manifestation of his glory in all his communicative attributes of power, wisdom, providence, and the rest, and that to the highest perfection that the most noble creatures, men, and angels can reach in order to honor and praise him in all his excellencies. Because anything in the creature is too base to be the ultimate and highest end of the Creator's actions. And to add anything to himself is impossible. Therefore, God's end remains only to be this relative respect between them that God's glory may be manifest in them and that the creatures may magnify him.

Fourthly, God's manifestation of his glory must not be in so easy and obvious a way that the shallow capacity of the choicest creatures may fully comprehend him and predict his ways. His hidden paths are infinitely beyond all his creatures finding out until he is pleased to manifest them, because ease and commonness strips things of admiration, exposing them to neglect and contempt.

Fifthly, to confound the wisdom of the wise, God employs such contrary and unlikely means to produce his ends that however much we think the work he does is impossible beforehand, so much more do we admire and esteem it afterward. Even if we slighted it before, we adore it afterward.

In these five conclusions stands a general rational account of God's actions. We observe all his works of wonder and miracles in Scripture – for example, leading Israel forty years through the wilderness (Exod. 12:37-38, Psa. 78:12) and Christ with his miraculous feeding of so many with so few loaves (John 6:5, Matt. 15:32). Are not God's ordinary works of nature as admirable? Even without the light of Scripture, heathen philosophers may conclude that doubtless there is one God whose universal and all powerful providence orders all things. One may reason concerning the conception of a child in the womb, as to who distributes that little mass of seed into flesh, skin and bone? Or being in this way changed, who causes it to branch forth into its head and members, with all their distinctions, rather than to congeal into a lump of bone wrapped in flesh, and covered over with skin? And why two arms and legs and only one body? Who branches forth the hands into five fingers with all their useful joints? Who distributes the internal organs, and gives life to all, with the faculty of growth, all in a due proportion? All of these are so far from the parent's power to dispose of, that they are often wholly ignorant of it, until it is brought forth. They do not have the power to choose to have male or female, proper, fair, or witty children, or any other such features. Further, divine design determines that eggs turn into chickens and acorns into oaks with such a certain rule, that doubtless they are from one overruling power of God. David sweetly meditates on the miracle of his own conception in Psalm 139:13-16. "For thou hast possessed my reins: thou hast covered me in my mother's womb. I will praise thee; for I am fearfully and wonderfully made: marvellous are thy works; and that my soul knoweth right well. My substance was not hid from thee, when I was made in secret, and curiously wrought in the lowest parts of the earth. Thine eyes did see my substance, yet being unperfect; and in thy book all my members were written, which in continuance were fashioned, when as yet there was none of them." And yet the miracle of human birth and creature continuance, because they are within the ordinary course of nature, are not always admired or esteemed and even little considered. So, it is true that familiarity breeds contempt. For it is as rare a work of God to turn water into wine by the ordinary course of nature, if you truly consider it, as it was for Christ to perform this miracle. For it is the nature of the vine to do it! Who gave it this nature and virtue? Sure, it is common and ordinary, but it is also so much the more admirable providentially because for so long this pattern has continued without fail. And to be sure, what is supported with constancy and certainty is wrought by wisdom and with power.

So, it is true. God could have, if he had so desired, prevented man's fall, Christ's death, and his children's sin and suffering. But then we would have failed to see the weakness of even the choicest of creatures, men, and angels, when not supported by God. We would not have experienced God's rich love in Christ as he was given a ransom for us, nor God's severe indignation against sin, his exacting of justice against reprobates, and his unfathomed free grace towards his elect. We would have missed his unblemished holiness that did not spare sin but found a way to punish it – in his children by way of chastisement and in his Son by way of satisfaction. We would not have experienced the power of the grace of God in his saints that is stronger than death, the very grace that works all things together for our good and with the best advantage for God's glory. We would have missed the opportunity to look with admiration into these paths of God, that we may say with Paul, "O the depth of the riches both of the wisdom and knowledge of God! How unsearchable are his judgments, and his ways past finding out! Who has known the mind of the Lord? For of him, and through him, and to him are all things. To him be glory forever. Amen!" (Rom. 11:33-36). Men cannot trace his paths or predict his ways because the end of all things is God's glory. He brings good out of evil, which could not be had if he did not first permit evil to exist. Paul's mention of such miraculous riddles and paradoxes in 2 Corinthians 6:4-10 tells us that the Spirit of God by faith acquaints his children with that which the natural man cannot discern. "But in all things approving ourselves as the ministers of God, in much patience, in afflictions, in necessities, in distresses, in stripes, in imprisonments, in tumults, in labours, in watchings, in fastings; by pureness, by knowledge, by longsuffering, by kindness, by the Holy Ghost, by love unfeigned, by the word of truth, by the power of God, by the armour of righteousness on the right hand and on the left, by honour and dishonour, by evil report and good report: as deceivers, and yet true; as unknown, and yet well known; as dying, and, behold, we live; as chastened, and not killed; as sorrowful, yet always rejoicing; as poor, yet making many rich; as having nothing, and yet possessing all things." Nothing so confounds Satan with all his assassins and foils him at his own weapon than allowing him to have his most malicious will, which in turn fully accomplishes God's own most holy will. A perfect example is that of Joseph when his brothers sold him as a slave. As Joseph relayed to them many, many years later, "You meant it for evil, but God meant it for good." Another example is that mighty man Samson, who was bound by the Philistines to deprive him of his strength, and in turn he exercised and evidenced his strength to their ruin. Yet another example is how David killed Goliath with his sling and several smooth stones from the brook, and so cut off Goliath's head with his own sword. In all Satan's attempts to bring Christ to death, the end result was to open the door to man's salvation and his own kingdom's desolation – the things Satan so feared and worked so hard to prevent. "Surely the wrath of man (and devils) shall praise thee, the remainder of wrath shalt thou restrain," (Psa. 76:10). That is, when God has allowed all the malice he intends to allow for his glory, he will dam up the residue. He will instantaneously put an end to it all when he is ready and his time is right, when God rises to judgement to save all the meek of the earth.

USE 1

The first application of this doctrine is to understand the several ways God has for delivering the godly from all their troubles.

1. God often smites the hearts of the enemies of his church and children with sudden fears of dangers to themselves, even when there is no cause, so that they run even when no one pursues them. This happened with the hosts of the Assyrians in 2 Kings 7:6-7 whom the Lord caused to hear a noise of chariots and horses, and of a great host, and so were utterly diverted. There are narratives of the enemy mistaking cattle for armies, rattling winds that strike horror, and another notable example of the Midianite's dream as told in Judges 7:13.

2. God often smites the enemies' hearts with relenting pity, making them prove to be friends to his church and children. Similarly, he turned Judah's and

Reuben's hearts towards Joseph to spare his life (Gen. 37:19). He turned the heart of King Ahasuerus towards Esther, reversing the sentence that would have destroyed the whole nation of the Jews (Esther 7). Similarly, Nebuchadnezzar's heart was set beforehand to free Daniel, and in the interim to be troubled for him (Daniel 6). These are examples of God's "preventing" ways of help.

    3. God often allows his churches and children's enemies to prosper in their malicious efforts and then, in turn, he confounds them and turns their designs to his own glory, the welfare of his church and children, and by it, to their enemies' shame and confusion. A prime example is found in the instances of Joseph's brethren who sold him into Egypt, the Philistines binding of Samson, and the betraying of the Christ to death. Another instance is when Saul gave Michal to David to be his wife in order to snare him with the dowry of a hundred of the Philistines' foreskins, that so David might fall under their hands. And yet this resulted in David's rise to greater honor (1 Sam. 18:22, *etc.*). Still another example is found in the accusers of the three Hebrew children (Daniel 3) and of Daniel himself, (Daniel 6), both which tended to the rise of them and the consequent ruin of their adversaries.

    4. God often leaves the principals alone, and only deals with the instruments of their cruelty, disabling them for service against his church and children. Such was the case with the fiery furnace and the lions in the two forenamed examples. Also, the chariot wheels of Pharaoh's host fell off in pursuit of Israel through the Red Sea, (Exod.

14:25). So, with the band of soldiers that came to arrest Jesus, as soon as he said, "I am he," they all went backward and fell to the ground (John 18:5-6). And the Apostle John, having been boiled in a cauldron of oil, came out without any injury.

5. God often allows the devil and all his instruments to do their worst, and then he does his best, his host against theirs, under whose command are all creatures. Some were so potent, in fact, that one angel in one night killed 185,000 enemies of his church (2 Kings 19:35). The stars in their courses fought against Sisera (Judges 5:20). The sun and moon stood still to give light to his people to be avenged of their enemies (Joshua 10:12-13). And God sent hosts of lice, flies, fleas, frogs, hail, death, and what not to punish kings for his people's sakes.

6. God often allows the wicked to prevail even to martyrdom against his church and his saints. But it is to free them from evils to come, to give them a more honorable crown of glory, and to raise up seed to his church from their blood. All these things are written for our instruction, for though we don't expect miraculous deliverances, as most of these were, yet through patience and comfort of the Scriptures we have hope that the Lord will find a way for us also to escape, based on his wise providence designed for his own glory and his children's good. For in the end he delivers them from eternal death and gives them life everlasting.

USE 2

God's children are men of observation, and as such we observe diligently God's gracious dealings both on behalf of his church, and to yourself in particular, to learn to praise him, to pray to him, and to trust in him. A great example is David, a man after God's own heart, who invoked songs of God's providence in all his wondrous works of grace to his church, historically from the beginning of the world down to his own times, and prophetically from his own time to the world's end. Therefore, the book of Psalms remains music for the church to the world's end.

USE 3

A third exhortation for the saints is that we be most deeply and chiefly troubled for our sins until we are pardoned of them on the merits of Christ and gain victory over them by the power of God's Spirit. This will alleviate all other troubles; they all will be easily overcome once our sin is rightly and thoroughly vanquished. That is when we experience joy in the Holy Spirit, not based on some false sense of eternal security and a veneer of forgiveness of sin, but because God is at home in our conscience. How sad is that man's condition who has no safety abroad nor quiet at home because of the sin that continually plagues his conscience. We carry this house, where conscience abides, wherever we go. For this reason, we should take heed how we deal with our sins. If we keep close tabs on our conscience to discover our sins early, then we may kill them. However, if they are allowed to remain and take root inside our heart, they put us at great risk, if God chooses not to show us mercy. Let our sins, therefore, be our greatest trouble. As Augustine says, "The carpenter hews timber which is rotten on the outside. But if he finds it sound within, he squares it and fits it for building, regardless of the outward unsound chips, which will be burned in the fire. It will profit us nothing to have sound bodies and hollow hearts with corrupted consciences, for these are the troubles which seize on us, that we sink under them. Get a good heart and a sound conscience, and in whatever troubles, you may retire and appeal to God with comfort, who will meet you there, speaking peace, no matter what troubles dog and pursue you from place to place. Otherwise, your sin will become your own accuser and tormentor, perpetually haunting you in every place and at every turn, and that much more fiercely for those secret, inner sins. And yet, even in these extremities, God, yes, God alone is our refuge," Augustine says, "He is our present help. Therefore, let us find out our sins, and with the help of our God, route them out, that they do not destroy us utterly." And let us make sure to have our God at peace within us. For though we are all born in our sins, yet take heed how we live in our sins, for then we shall die in our sins. The sin nature is with the godly until death, yet they are not in their sins, but in Christ Jesus. They are new creatures, continually mortifying all their sinful lusts. O let it be so with me, and with you also, whoever you are, as we nurture the eternal salvation of our souls.

USE 4

In this fourth exhortation, we rest upon God alone for delivery in all our troubles. Isaiah 26:3-4 speaks fully to this purpose. "Thou wilt keep him in perfect peace, whose mind is stayed on thee: because he trusteth in thee. Trust ye in the LORD for ever: for in the LORD JEHOVAH is everlasting strength." Let no carnal reasonings draw us away from our repose in God. We can secure ourselves and take refuge and comfort in God's all-powerful, wise, and good providence, for we know that God disposes of kings and kingdoms, bringing down one and setting up another. He does whatever he pleases, both in heaven and on earth.

Secondly, we should know that God is not fickle, but sparing and forbearing until our sins so provoke him that the honor of all his glorious attributes like justice, truth, and holiness are so deeply engaged that he must avenge his anger and render justice. He spared the Canaanites until their sins were ripe for judgment. Judah's sins grew to the measure for which there was no remedy (2 Chron. 36:16). "Fill ye up the measure of your fathers," (Matt. 23:32). "A fruitful land he turns into barrenness, for the iniquity of them that dwell therein," (Psa. 107:34).

Thirdly, we should know further that in all these catastrophes God still preserves his church (the city of God and the kingdom of Christ) safe and sound, though he may move his candlestick from one nation to another. Though all Judea and Palestine were laid waste, the church settled in Greece. And when it was overrun, it moved into these western and northern territories, and happily it took its flight into America. And certainly, it will not be extinct until the world's end, and not even then, because it will be perfected in heaven.

Lastly, we should know that in all these relocations God took special care of his chosen ones (those who are his true church). Therefore, even temporal governments (much less Christ's church), do not depend on fate, human strength, or policy, but on God's most wise and just providence and grace. Therefore, let no such vain conceit deflect us from making God our God, our hope, refuge, and shelter, in whom we shall find a very present, great, and abundant help in our ever so present, great, and abundant troubles. Labor to make God your God, by giving him all you possibly can. Break off all associations with sin, because until this is done, there is no coming to God; he does not *listen to those who continue in their sin.* "He that turneth away his ear from hearing the law, even his prayer shall be abomination," (Prov. 28:9).

Secondly, do not seek other helpers but rely on him only, fully trusting him in the ways and means which he prescribes and allows. God is jealous. He will have no rival for our heart. He who works all in all must be to you all in all. "For of him, and through him, and to him are all things, to him be all praise for ever," (Rom. 11:36).

Thirdly, to this end celebrate all his former great deliverances for his church and chosen. And be like David who tuned his heart to sing praises to God for past victories!

Fourthly, let faith infer from what God has done to what he both can and will do in the future. He who is the same without change, if his wisdom sees cause, his goodness will do it. Therefore, strengthen your faith, comfort your spirit, take courage to endeavor. As David argued, "God delivered me from the lion, and the bear," (1 Sam. 17:34-35, *cf.* 2 Cor. 1:10), "Therefore will he also deliver me from this uncircumcised Philistine." And as Paul declares, "God has delivered us, and does deliver us, in whom we trust that he will deliver us."

Fifthly, be fervent, and frequent God by prayer in all your troubles. Season your prayers with salty tears of repentance for your sins, which provoke him to trouble us.

Lastly, (1 Kings 21:29)[3] by faith, prayer, praise, repentance, and obedience, make God your hope, refuge, and shelter, not only in times of trouble but also in times of peace. Seek him in the height of prosperity, as you look for his help in the depth of adversity. In this way, God will not seem strange, nor look strange on you when you come to him, but you may rather have gained his care and favor and free recourse in your time of need. Likewise, in this way you may prevent rather than remove troubles, which is the

---

[3] "Seest thou how Ahab humbleth himself before me? because he humbleth himself before me, I will not bring the evil in his days: but in his son's days will I bring the evil upon his house," (1 Kings 21:29).

easier task. God does not need to prescribe a remedy if you have no illness. One or other greater distemper may be recovered by speedy repentance, in such case God will not need to prescribe any bitter medicine or apply any painful discipline.

Finally, I say, discharge the duty, which this our text prescribes, and you may confidently infer that you need not fear, though the earth be removed.

May God Almighty's blessings be yours.

FINIS.

Other Helpful Works Published by Puritan Publications

A Call to Delaying Sinners
by Thomas Doolittle (1632–1707)

Taking Hold of Eternal Life in Christ
by George Gifford (1547-1620)

The Victorious Christian Soldier in Christ's Army
by Urian Oakes (1631–1681)

The Believer's Marriage with Christ
by Michael Harrison (1640-1729)

*Discerning the Signs of the Times
and the Church's Reformation*
by Samuel Willard (1640-1707)

Zeal for God's House Quickened
by Oliver Bowles B.D. (1574-1664?)

Resisting the Devil with a Steadfast Faith
by George Gifford (1547-1620)

The Doctrine of Man's Future Eternity
by John Jackson (1600-1648)

A Treatise of the Loves of Christ to His Spouse

God is Our Refuge and Our Strength
by Samuel Bolton, D.D. (1606-1654)

Faith, Election and the Believer's Assurance
by George Gifford (1547-1620)

The Sovereign Efficacy of Divine Providence
by Urian Oakes (1631–1681)

God's Afflicting Providence, and Other Works
by Francis Roberts (1609-1675)

*The Vision of the Wheels:
A Treatise on the Providence of God*
by Matthew Mead (1630-1699)

Joseph's Resolve and the Unreasonableness of Sinning Against God
by C. Matthew McMahon

The Glorious Name of God the Lord of Hosts
by Jeremiah Burroughs (1599-1646)

Christian Truths Necessary for Salvation
by Nicholas Byfield (1579–1622)

The Christian's Duty and Safety in Evil Times
by Christopher Love (1618-1651)

www.ingramcontent.com/pod-product-compliance
Lightning Source LLC
LaVergne TN
LVHW051528070426
835507LV00023B/3376